Debunking Conspiracy Theories

Anna Maria Johnson

Cavendish
Square

New York

Published in 2019 by Cavendish Square Publishing, LLC
243 5th Avenue, Suite 136, New York, NY 10016

Library of Congress Cataloging-in-Publication Data

Names: Johnson, Anna Maria, author.
Title: Debunking conspiracy theories / Anna Maria Johnson.
Description: First edition. | New York, NY : Cavendish Square Publishing,
LLC, 2019. | Series: News literacy | Summary: "A book for young
readers about the concept of conspiracy theories and the critical thinking
used to understand and unravel them"-- Provided by publisher. |
Includes bibliographical references and index. | Audience: Young readers.
Identifiers: LCCN 2018013752 (print) | LCCN 2018025139
(ebook) | ISBN 9781502640499 (ebook) | ISBN 9781502640482
(library bound) | ISBN 9781502640475 (pbk.)
Subjects: LCSH: Conspiracy theories--Juvenile literature.
| Media literacy--Juvenile literature.
Classification: LCC HV6275 (ebook) | LCC HV6275 .J64 2019 (print) | DDC 001.9--dc23
LC record available at https://lccn.loc.gov/2018013752

Editorial Director: David McNamara
Editor: Caitlyn Miller
Copy Editor: Lisa Goldstein
Associate Art Director: Alan Sliwinski
Designer: Joe Parenteau
Production Coordinator: Karol Szymczuk
Photo Research: J8 Media

The photographs in this book are used by permission and through the courtesy of: Cover U.S. Army photo by
Capt. Richard Barker/Wikimedia Commons/File:25th CAB trains with Navy divers 130619AAB123068. jpg/Public
Domain; p. 4 Twin Design/Shutterstock.com; p. 7 Tata Donets/Shutterstock.com; p. 8 Ded Mityay/Shutterstock.
com; p. 10 Brooks Kraft/ Getty Images; p. 11 Chris Harvey/Shutterstock.com; p. 12 Lisa F. Young/Shutterstock.
com; p. 14 Oscity/Shutterstock.com; p. 19 Justin Sullivan/Getty Images; p. 20 Courtesy Nitya Parthasarathy;
p. 21 Dan Callister/Getty Images; p. 23 Yuri Samsonov/Shutterstock.com; p. 25 Mark Wilson/Getty Images; p. 26
B Christopher/Alamy Stock Photo; p. 27 (left) Ullstein Bild/Getty Images, (right) Library of Congress/Wikimedia
Commons/File:William Randolph Hearst cph.3b30409.jpg/Public Domain; p. 28 Chuck Wagner/Shutterstock.
com; p. 30 Darren Baker/Shutterstock.com; p. 39 Courtesy The News Literacy Project; p. 40 Africa Studio/
Shutterstock.com; p. 43 Ken Wolter/Shutterstock.com; p. 45 Peter Macdiarmid/Getty Images; p. 47 Katherine
Welles/Shutterstock.com; p. 49 Sandy Stifler/Shutterstock.com; p. 53 Andrey Armyagov/Shutterstock.com.

Printed in the United States of America

CONTENTS

The internet has allowed information to travel faster and farther than ever before. That means conspiracy theories can now spread faster too.

What Are Conspiracy Theories?

A conspiracy is a plot between two or more people to trick others. A theory is a complex idea that involves many pieces coming together to form an explanation about something. A theory has not yet been proven. Taken together, then, a conspiracy theory is a story that tries to explain how two or more people are working together to trick or plot against others—but the claim has not been proven. Some common conspiracy theories are about people in government trying to trick citizens. Others are about medical or health care workers tricking patients. Often a conspiracy theory is about two or more people with power using the theory to fool people with less power. With the rise of the information age, conspiracy theories are circulated faster than ever.

YouTube, Facebook, and many other websites create equal opportunities for both information and misinformation to spread. Many conspiracy theories are based on misinformation rather than actual facts.

True or False?

Conspiracy theories can be true or false. Sometimes a conspiracy theory is proven correct, and then it becomes part of history. An example of this from American history is the Watergate scandal from President Nixon's era. At first, there were rumors that a 1972 robbery at the Watergate building complex was connected to a government conspiracy. In the beginning, the White House denied the connection. Later, evidence was found that showed President Nixon knew about the robbery. He also knew about some wiretapping activities, which is a way of spying on phone calls. After officials discovered more evidence from these scandals, President Nixon resigned. He is the only United States president to have done so. When a conspiracy theory is proven correct, it is usually through a process of investigation. Investigative journalism is when journalists or reporters do a lot of work to uncover the truth. Congressional investigations are when government officials, such as members of Congress, uncover the truth. Watergate was discovered by both journalists and Congress.

At other times a conspiracy theory can be "debunked," or shown to be untrue. An example of a debunked conspiracy theory is the belief that astronauts did not set foot on the moon. There is a lot of evidence that

CAUTION
Conspiracy Theory Ahead

Internet users need to proceed carefully when reading online. Not everything found on the internet is true or reliable.

twelve astronauts have gone to the moon, which proved this theory wrong.

Often, however, a conspiracy theory remains mysterious and cannot be proven true or untrue. People might never know for sure the circumstances that led to the death of actress Marilyn Monroe. The official version is strong, but so are personal accounts that contradict that version.

As readers and consumers of information, students today have the fascinating—and sometimes difficult—job of sorting out which theories are likely to be true, false, or uncertain.

The Appeal of Conspiracy Theories

Maybe you or someone you know enjoys finding and thinking about conspiracy theories. These theories can be very interesting because they ask us to think about the world in a different way than other people think about it. Conspiracy theories are also interesting because they make us look for patterns and connections. Finding patterns or fitting together the pieces of a puzzle is satisfying to many people. Conspiracy theories are usually surprising, and most people enjoy new ideas. In today's information-rich culture, it is good to be skeptical about what we read. Conspiracy theories play an important role in teaching us to be skeptical.

Historian Kathryn S. Olmsted, who teaches about American history and government at a university in California, says, "Conspiracy theories are easy ways of telling complicated stories." The real world is a complicated place, but people feel uncomfortable when they don't understand how complex things work. It feels good to have a simple story to explain what is otherwise mind-boggling. Olmsted and other experts have studied conspiracy theories and why people are attracted to them. There are many reasons why people believe in conspiracy theories. One reason is that some people want to feel part of a certain group. They will agree with the group's unproven ideas in order

Dollar bills include the Great Seal of the United States, presented to Congress in 1782 by Charles Thomson. There are many conspiracy theories about the "true meaning" of the symbols on the Great Seal.

DEMANDING EXTRAORDINARY EVIDENCE

Well-known American astronomer and scientist Carl Sagan said, "Extraordinary claims require extraordinary evidence." This means that the more surprising the claim, the more evidence is needed to prove it. While some conspiracy theories turn out to have merit, many never offer enough evidence to prove their claims. It is best to be wary or skeptical of theories that don't have many strong facts to support them. In the past, when conspiracy theories have proved to be true, there were hundreds of boxes filled with evidence to prove the case, as in Watergate.

to belong. In other cases, people distrust authority such as the government. They believe that powerful people are covering up the truth from the public. And, as mentioned before, some conspiracy theories in the past have proved to be true.

Unfortunately, some people are just looking for a chance to make money. They invent conspiracy theories and use them to sell products. For example, one popular website posts stories and conspiracy theories to make people worry about the future. The InfoWars website has an online store that sells emergency food, survival gear, and other supplies. Readers who believe the scary stories and articles then buy the expensive emergency supplies. The website owner, Alex Jones, makes money. Alex Jones

Alex Jones is an American talk show host and a popular conspiracy theorist. In July 2016, he spoke at a rally to support Donald Trump's presidential campaign.

has been called the leading conspiracy theorist in America. His website does not follow the best guidelines for careful news reporting practices. Those guidelines will be discussed later in this book.

Harmful Effects

Conspiracy theories can cause a variety of problems. They can cause people to doubt authority figures and experts. They can also prevent people from taking positive actions to combat a real problem that is incorrectly labeled as a conspiracy theory. Often, conspiracy theories are not based on well-founded evidence and logic. Instead, many conspiracy theories are based on logical fallacies, which are gaps in logical thinking. The consequences of conspiracy theories can be big or small, depending on the situation.

A major consequence of conspiracy theories is that people start to lose trust in institutions. Institutions include the health care system, the government, and science-based organizations. When this happens, people may not get the care they need. For example, one common conspiracy theory is that vaccines cause autism. When this idea was first introduced and then spread, many parents did not immunize their children. As a result, in parts of the country where children were not vaccinated, diseases broke out, including whooping cough and mumps.

Perhaps one of the greatest challenges we face today is the problem of global climate change. Some people say that climate change is a conspiracy theory. This has led to inaction and a lack of problem-solving. In order to tackle big problems, people have to trust one another and use their best thinking skills to find accurate information and solutions.

There are also conspiracy theories that are harmless, however. For example, some people believe that aliens have visited Earth, and those visits were covered up. A belief like this doesn't cause harm to anyone and might be entertaining or fun to think about.

Stories about aliens and UFOs have fascinated people for decades. These stories are mostly harmless.

Teachers and librarians are helpful resources as students learn how to judge the quality of online information.

More Common Than Ever

Although conspiracy theories are not new, they are more abundant now than ever before. The growth of the internet and information age means that more people are able to spread their ideas widely without fact-checkers or experts to verify the information they are posting. As a result, it can be hard for ordinary people to weed out the myths from the reliable material available online. Librarians and other information experts have put together resources and checklists to help the general population sift through information. We are likely to find a new conspiracy theory any time we use the internet, so it is important to be able to evaluate how plausible the story might be.

A FLAT EARTH?

Earth is a planet that orbits the sun. This is supported with facts and scientific evidence. Even ancient Greeks and Romans used math to figure out the shape of Earth. Christopher Columbus and others who explored the world by ship in the 1400s knew they could not fall off Earth. Satellites take daily pictures of Earth so that we can see weather patterns and use accurate maps. Today, astronauts who live in the International Space Station have a beautiful view of our blue and green ball-shaped planet.

Yet a small number of people today believe Earth is flat. They say the globe is a conspiracy by the government. They claim that all the pictures of Earth are altered using software. They think that all GPS devices are rigged. "Flat Earthers" have gained a following recently. This is because of the internet, which spreads stories quickly to a large audience. The Flat Earth Society has a website that spreads its ideas. They convince about two hundred people per year, including some celebrities.

Rapper Bobby Ray Simmons Jr. (B.o.B.) created a song called "Flatline" in which he disagrees with astrophysicist Neil deGrasse Tyson. Simmons thinks the horizon looks like a straight line. Former NBA basketball player Shaquille O'Neal also claimed Earth was flat, but he later said he was joking.

Librarians and experts recommend that we trust the opinions of experts over celebrities. They also point out that even if someone is an expert in one area, that person might not be knowledgeable in other areas. For example, Shaq is credible when it comes to basketball plays. But Tyson and other scientists are more credible when it comes to the shape of the planet.

Mandalay Bay Resort and Casino in Las Vegas was the site of a mass shooting in 2017. Many conspiracy theories spread widely after the shooting.

Characteristics of Conspiracy Theories

Many internet users have had the experience of looking for information through Google or another search engine and finding some very odd results. For example, after a major event like a natural disaster or tragedy, some of the reported stories about the event will later turn out to have been false. After the mass shooting at a Las Vegas concert in 2017, some sources reported multiple shooters when there was really only one man. Sometimes a combination of false and true stories will grow into a conspiracy theory related to the event. With practice, readers can become skilled at identifying a conspiracy theory. There are a number of characteristics that make it obvious that a story is a conspiracy theory.

Again, it is worth noting that some conspiracy theories do turn out to be true. But many others stick around for years after they have been debunked. It is this second group that is worthy of concern. Readers and internet users need to be able to identify conspiracy theories and determine whether or not they have merit.

Too Shocking to Be True

There is an old expression, "If it sounds too good to be true, it might not be true." Sometimes the truth can be surprising or even shocking, but it is wise to ask for more evidence whenever a theory doesn't seem very likely.

If a theory puts down or is suspicious of expert opinions, it is usually best not to trust that theory. For example, one common headline on the internet reads, "Doctors don't want you to know about this miracle cure!" In reality, most experts choose to enter a field because they want to make life better for others. They want to study that field more deeply and share their knowledge. Therefore, most experts do not want to hide the truths and cures that they find. If there is a miracle cure, most doctors would want their patients to be able to try it.

Another tip-off that something might be a conspiracy theory is the use of overgeneralizations. An overgeneralization is when someone describes many things in the same way without noticing small differences. For example, if someone ate a new food and did not like it, it would be an overgeneralization to say that he or she hates to try new foods. A common example of an overgeneralization is when conspiracy theorists refer to "the government." The government includes many different branches and thousands of people working together. There are different levels of government including local, state (or provincial), and national. Conspiracy theories lump all these different levels and people together as if they were one.

Bias

Bias is something to watch for as well. Bias means that the story takes one perspective without considering another view or side. Some news sources are guilty of representing one political party kindly while showing the other party to be foolish or mean. In the United States, the two-party system (in which Democrats and Republicans are the two primary political parties) sometimes creates the opportunity for news sources or others to take one party's view at the expense of the other. Canada has more than two political parties, but bias can still be a problem there as well. While it is fine to decide that one view makes a stronger case than the other, the decision should be made after respectfully considering all voices.

Other types of bias matter too. Gender bias occurs when an article or news source promotes stereotypes about men and women. It can also refer to representing one gender over another. For example, a biased article might quote only men, even when qualified women could have been interviewed. Recently, as women have found more chances to work and to serve in government, conspiracy theories have cropped up around gender. Men who feel threatened by women in power promote these

ALGORITHMS AT LARGE

Thanks to the power of the internet, most of us are likely to get our news from online sources instead of a print newspaper. As a result, big technology companies are able to measure very precisely which stories get the most attention. Then the computers promote those stories, which means these articles are more likely to turn up in the next person's search results. This process uses algorithms, or computer-made codes, to influence what news stories show up the most on the internet. The codes don't know how to judge truth or quality of the stories, as a human being could. Instead, the codes are based on the popularity of the story, article, or website. Therefore, search engines like Google often show stories that promote conspiracy theories more often than the reputable sites that debunk them. This is a problem because more people are reading about conspiracy theories than about critical thinking.

Most search engine algorithms are designed to find sources based on internet traffic patterns rather than credibility or reliability. The *Guardian* reported that "After the Las Vegas shooting that killed 58 people and injured hundreds more, videos falsely claiming the attack was a 'hoax' ... earned millions of views on YouTube, causing great distress to those affected." But in the future, search engine companies could improve their algorithms so that more trustworthy sites turn up on the first page of results instead of what has the most shock value or clicks. Some information leaders are taking action already. After the Las Vegas conspiracy videos, YouTube adjusted its search algorithms. However, the spread of false

Susan Wojcicki, CEO of YouTube, announced in 2018 that the organization will take steps to reduce the spread of conspiracy theories through its channels.

news after a big event remains a problem. New strategies to promote legitimate news are still needed.

YouTube is stepping up. CEO of YouTube, Susan Wojcicki, announced on March 14, 2018, that the platform would take new action to solve its conspiracy theory problem. One idea is to include a link to a Wikipedia article next to each conspiracy theory post to provide context for the theory.

Critics say this strategy might not work if conspiracy theorists edit the Wikipedia article to match their theories instead of other known facts. Even Wikipedia says it is not designed to handle breaking news events. It is designed to develop slowly, over time.

conspiracy theories online. Bias can also come out as stereotypes related to certain religions, ethnicities, or other categories. Some negative conspiracy theories focus around a bias against a certain group of people. There are conspiracy theories related to Catholics, Jews, and Muslims, to name a few.

An American high school student created an algorithm to try to identify gender bias in news articles. Nitya Parthasarathy goes to school in Irvine, California. Her program allows anyone to upload a document and have it scored for bias.

Nitya Parthasarathy, an American high school student, created an algorithm to help identify bias in news stories.

Gaps and Context

Sometimes conspiracy theories seem to have a carefully worked out logic in which all pieces of the theory work together. Sometimes, however, the logic is limited and only works when important context is left out. Some people believe that a region in Nevada's Mojave Desert, known as Area 51, is a place where aliens landed during the 1950s. What is known for sure is that Area 51 was where the US military tested more than one hundred nuclear bombs and other military projects in the 1950s. Aliens may be more interesting than weapons, but since the 1950s, the world has seen plenty of evidence of nuclear power and no evidence of aliens. In recent years, government documents that used to be secret have been declassified, or made available to the public. These documents explain what actually happened in Area 51.

Yet some people are so convinced by their favorite conspiracy theory that no amount of evidence or logic will change their minds. This leads us to another trait of hardened conspiracy theories—an

This sign stands near the border of Area 51, a US military base in Nevada, where people claim to have seen UFOs and other strange sights.

unwillingness to look at new evidence. If a conspiracy theory is a good one, then it will stand up to new tests and new evidence. But if a conspiracy theorist is not interested or willing to believe in other possibilities, that is a sign that the conspiracy theory may not be worth considering.

Why People Continue to Believe Debunked Conspiracy Theories

If conspiracy theories are often proven false, and if they can be identified using the above tips and strategies, then why do people still promote them? There are a few reasons for that as well. One reason is that people genuinely believe them. Many people—even adults—understand a little bit of science, but not a lot. That puts them at risk of believing a theory that sounds scientific even if they don't understand the details.

For example, fluoride is something that dentists believe strengthens teeth when administered in an appropriate amount. Numerous reputable studies support this, which is why many cities add fluoride to the water supply. On the other hand, too much fluoride can make a person sick. Yet the amount of fluoride it takes to make someone sick is far more than what anyone could drink in water! People who don't have a solid understanding of fluoride dosages might be afraid of drinking water with fluoride in it. These people might say their city leadership is conspiring to make citizens sick with the fluoridated water.

A good way to debunk this conspiracy theory would be to study the science behind fluoride. Furthermore, one could compare the health rates of people who live in

Fluoride is often added to tap water in the United States. Fluoridated water is not harmful, even though conspiracy theories say it is.

cities with fluoridated water and those who live in cities without it. Has anyone gotten sick from drinking the water with fluoride? Another way to think about the conspiracy theory is to ask, why would the leaders of the city want to make people sick? Making citizens sick is likely to get them in a lot of trouble and would not benefit them in any way. Therefore, it is unlikely that the city leadership is conspiring against its own people.

Alternatively, there have been a few cases where cities have made bad decisions about the water supply, and citizens have gotten sick. In Flint, Michigan, people got sick not from fluoride in the water but from lead. Scientists know that lead in water makes people sick and does not have any health benefits. In the city of Flint, Michigan, large amounts of lead contaminated the water supply starting in 2014, and people got very sick. It is important to point out that the local leaders did not plan for people to get sick, but they did make bad choices about how to take care of the water supply in order to save money. When an event like extreme water contamination happens, it is difficult to keep it a secret. The story from

WHO'S GOT THE POWER?

Paul Ratner, who writes for the website Big Think, wrote an article called "America's Ten Most Popular Conspiracy Theories." This article named scientific studies that have revealed some of the factors that lead people to believe in superstitions and unproven conspiracy theories. College professors Jennifer Whitson and Adam Galinksy studied this topic a decade ago. Whitson and Galinsky set up an experiment that involved putting people in different situations where they were given different amounts of control. Then Whitson and Galinsky showed the participants pictures and asked them to describe what they saw. People who had been given less control were later more likely to imagine they saw things in the pictures that were not really there. This experiment and five other experiments Whitson and Galinsky conducted suggested that people who felt like they had less control were more likely to see things that were not there. These people were then more likely to look for explanations through superstition and conspiratorial explanations.

On a positive note, after the first part of the experiment, some of the people were given a chance to feel more in control. These people then became less likely to see patterns and images that were not really there. Whitson and Galinsky's work echoes what Paul Ratner says about why so many people believe conspiracy theories.

Jessica Owens from Flint, Michigan, showed a bottle of her contaminated water to members of Congress on February 3, 2016. She asked for help to end the water crisis in Flint.

Flint, Michigan, made news across the country and prompted change. The city provided bottled water and water filters for residents to use.

When one city does a bad job, however, those who hear about it might become more suspicious of their own elected leaders. They feel that if one city made bad choices about its water treatment plans, then other cities might make bad decisions too. In such cases, conspiracy theories gain strength because people feel that all city officials are not trustworthy. We know that leaders *can* and *have* taken harmful actions—but that does not mean that every conspiracy will turn out to be true.

Follow the Money

Sometimes conspiracy theories are spread by people who may not even believe them. This is because of a profit motive to spread interesting or shocking tales, even if they are not confirmed.

Unfortunately, some newspapers and websites make their money by shocking or scaring readers. When people

Advertisements are on much of the print and online media we see each day. The desire to sell ads can make news sources and websites publish sensational stories.

read a sensational headline or title, they are more likely to click on that and read the story. Then the newspaper or website can get more advertisers. These types of websites and news sources spread unproven theories to more people than other sources that are worded more carefully. Even before the internet age, print newspapers and magazines used shocking or misleading headlines to sell more copies of their publications. This practice was very common in the 1890s and was called yellow journalism. Two different New York City newspapers, one run by William Randolph Hearst and the other by Joseph Pulitzer, competed with each other for readers by printing sensationalist stories. Historians say yellow journalism was one factor that led to the Spanish-American War because many of the news stories had an anti-Spain bias. After the battle between these two newspapers died down around the turn of the twentieth century, some yellow journalism practices remained. Since the internet age, however, the number of magazines, newspapers, and other kinds of media has increased. As the number of media sources increase, so does the competition between them. Each races to sell as many stories as possible.

Making money from newspapers and magazines is not a bad thing. But the desire to sell copies can tempt some writers and editors to be careless with the truth. Instead of using careful words like "seem" or "might," titles will sound more confident than they should. Conspiracy theories, as mentioned before, are very interesting and appealing to many people, so focusing on them can boost sales.

Joseph Pulitzer (*left*) and William Randolph Hearst (*right*) owned rival American newspapers and both printed sensational stories as they competed for ad money.

Readers can get around this problem by sticking to news sources that make their money in a different way. Some of the best newspapers are funded through subscriptions instead of (or in addition to) advertisements. When that is the case, journalists have more reason to write clearly and truthfully, instead of reporting what is likely to attract more attention. Mainstream newspapers such as the *Washington Post, New York Times, LA Times*, and other city newspapers usually have a strong subscription base. When readers subscribe, they are paying the newspaper to do the work of good journalism. This leaves the newspapers less vulnerable to shock tactics. Although ads appear in these newspapers too, the ads are more likely to come from reputable companies and businesses rather than false or misleading sources.

The Role of Social Media and Other Digital Platforms

Since conspiracy theories often take a complicated, mysterious topic and oversimplify it, these theories spread quickly online through social media. GIFs, memes, Twitter posts, and other digital formats and platforms spread conspiracy theories faster than print publications could. Facebook groups can form around a particular conspiracy theory and allow those who believe it to connect with others around the world who believe it too. Then the theories seem more likely because social media users can surround themselves with other people who think the same way.

GIFs and memes are effective at spreading ideas quickly without inspiring much critical thinking. This could be seen as a pro or a con. The ideas, if they are good ones like the importance of washing your hands when you have a cough, can get out to the public in an effective way. On the other hand, a weak, false, or even harmful idea that is packaged into a cute or funny GIF or meme can also spread quickly. Viral videos spread conspiracy theories across YouTube, Facebook, and other platforms where users are very likely to see them.

Conspiracy theories can show up in print publications, too, but the process takes much longer than publishing them online. Before the internet became widespread, conspiracy theories were spread by word of mouth, usually from one person to a few others at a time. Sometimes they were spread through pamphlets or newspapers. Now, a conspiracy theory can be spread around the world with the click of a button.

A medical expert tests blood as part of her research. Look for experts' opinions as you evaluate conspiracy theories.

Fighting Conspiracy Theories

Some surprising events from history began as conspiracy theories that were later proven to be historical fact. But many of the common conspiracy theories on the internet today are based on misinformation. They often lack logic. These should not be taken seriously. Luckily, there are ways to fight conspiracy theories that have been proven false yet continue to spread. It is important for internet users to stop the spread of false information and harmful theories.

Tips and Strategies for Debunking Conspiracy Theories

False conspiracy theories can be debunked or discredited. Many common theories have already been tested by experts or government officials to see if they are true. A little sleuthing can uncover these investigations. However, false theories don't always go away when they are found to be false. The internet and other media have a way of keeping these theories alive to cause trouble for years afterward.

Use Sound Logic

Conspiracy theories can easily draw people in. But critical thinking skills can help readers see when this is happening. One valuable way to develop critical thinking skills is to study the rules of logic. These rules of logic go back at least two thousand years to the time of the ancient Greeks and Romans. One famous thinker named Aristotle wrote about logic and rhetoric. Rhetoric is the skill of making a good argument or case for something. Aristotle's rules of logic and rhetoric are still used today.

Something to watch for in your news sources and conspiracy theories is the use of logic. Every good theory needs good evidence (facts). But facts are not enough on their own. The theory also needs a rationale, or a careful explanation of how the facts fit together to support the theory. A poorly developed theory will leave gaps between the facts (evidence) and the rationale. It might rely on logical fallacies (or poor logic).

For example, it is a fact that during summertime, people eat more ice cream. Also during summer, there is an increase in the number of people who drown in lakes and oceans. These two facts are both true. But it would be poor logic to say that eating ice cream is what causes people to drown. It would be even less logical to claim

HEROES OF INFORMATION

Changes in technology have led to changes in how information is shared. Today low-quality information is spread as easily as high-quality information. This new development in our culture presents a chance to make new tools that can help improve the quality of the news and other information available to readers.

One group of people who have the job of sorting through information to find the best quality sources are librarians. Librarians spend years studying information, credibility, and how to evaluate books, newspapers, and online sources for quality.

Similarly, journalists spend years studying how to write news stories. Many journalists attend graduate schools, where they learn the best practices for fact-checking and reporting. Good journalists and newspapers will follow a code of ethics. A code of ethics is a set of rules to guide good behavior and practices. Some rules that journalists should follow are to report without bias, to provide context for quotations, to check facts before printing their stories, and to provide names and sources of where they got their information. If they make a mistake, they must publish corrections to fix their errors.

Librarians and properly trained journalists are on the frontlines of fighting misinformation. Some of the organizations that work to further that mission are the Poynter Institute, Columbia Journalism School, and the American Library Association. The best-trained journalists and librarians follow these organizations' recommendations and ethics codes.

that drowning causes people to eat ice cream. Although both facts relate to summer, we cannot assume that one causes the other.

A better rationale would be to point out that when the weather is hot, people are more likely to want to swim. When people swim, they have a higher chance of drowning. When the weather is hot, people are also more likely to crave ice cream. But there is not a direct cause-and-effect relationship between eating ice cream and drowning. The cause of both is warm weather. Some conspiracy theories include real facts but put them together in faulty ways.

The Buck Stops Here

Although most people who talk about conspiracy theories truly believe them, there are some who will spread ideas even if they don't believe them. They do this just to earn money. A good question to ask when looking at a conspiracy theory is: Might there be a profit motive? Is someone making money by sharing this new or unusual information? If so, does this change how it should be viewed?

When reading a news or magazine article, it can be helpful to notice what else is on the page. The content that goes around the article is called paratext. Paratext can include advertisements, sidebars, images and illustrations, and captions. The most professional sources, such as textbooks, often do not have advertisements at all. But because printing and publishing is expensive, ads are common in most news sources.

Next, one might ask, what kinds of products are being sold? What do the ads suggest about the intended audience? For example, magazines about geography often include ads about traveling to exotic places. Fitness magazines include ads for workout wear and sneakers. Business magazines usually run ads for suits, dress shirts, and airplane tickets. Readers can examine the ads to see what the magazine or newspaper assumes about its audience. If the ads are for products that are low quality or don't work, that reflects poorly on the magazine or newspaper.

If a website is selling weapons and survivalist gear, what might that suggest about the website's credibility? What kind of articles would a reader expect to find on such a website? What might a reader assume or guess about the people who read that website?

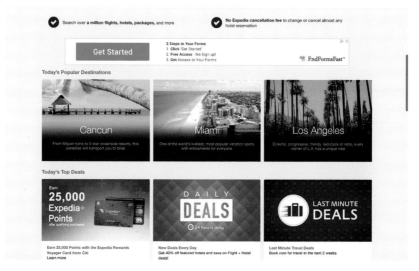

This screenshot of a website shows an example of paratext. In this case, the paratext includes travel advertisements.

Compare and Contrast

Another strategy for evaluating conspiracy theories is to read articles from several different sources or sites. Then readers can compare and contrast what is presented in each of them. If a widely accepted source like the BBC presents different information than a lesser-known source, readers will need to use critical thinking skills to determine which is more likely to be true.

When it comes to health-related topics, a reader might compare the new information with what other generally accepted sources state. For example, what do the Centers for Disease Control and Prevention and the World Health Organization have to say about health-related conspiracy topics? Readers can also compare sources from different countries' governments to see if they agree or disagree.

Perhaps the best strategy of all is to read broadly. Generally, it is not good practice to trust only one newspaper or source for information. If a person reads a wide variety of materials, he or she will notice if one source doesn't match the others. By reading many different kinds of books, articles, and magazines, a reader develops critical thinking skills for evaluating just about any material.

In particular, a reader might explore what other experts in the field think about the conspiracy. If just one doctor is alarmed about a cancer cure conspiracy, but other doctors think that one is incorrect, then the general public is safer believing the majority of doctors over the one raising alarm.

After reading a variety of other sources, the reader can go back to the conspiracy theory and evaluate whether it might be legitimate. Things to keep in mind are: Have the conspiracy theory's claims been tested? If so, what were the results? Is the person promoting the conspiracy really an expert? Do they have credentials and experience that makes them trustworthy? What is motivating this person to spread the theory?

Study the Real Deal

One of the best ways to identify and debunk unfounded conspiracy theories is to spend time studying truthful, good quality news sources. If you are used to seeing articles and stories presented in a professional, unbiased way with strong logic and support, then the fake stories will jump out at you.

People who study forged (or fake) money and art say that the best way to identify a fake is to know the real thing. It is the same with information. If you spend most of your time looking at good quality information, then when you see something of low quality, you will learn to notice it.

A good quality source will identify the author. It will often include a biography to explain why the author has experience in the appropriate topic. Good sources will acknowledge where they got their information. They do this by citing sources and naming the people they interview. Often well-reported stories will include hyperlinks to help the reader find more credible information about the topic. Trustworthy reporters will try to write in a style that sounds fair and not biased. If the source is an article in a newspaper or magazine, a reader can do a little research to see if the newspaper or magazine has a good reputation. Websites will include contact information so that curious readers can write to the author or organization. Responsible websites and newspapers will provide information about their mission, history, and ethics. If the source is connected to a respected university or government organization, it is probably trustworthy.

There are so many good sources of information available today through print, the internet, and many other sources. Librarians can help readers find the best quality information. Ethics codes can give us rules to observe. Students and readers of all ages should try to stay away from news and information sources that use biased language, shocking headlines and titles, or that don't provide where they got their information.

Fighting the Good Fight

All readers and citizens have a responsibility to try to stop the spread of poor or false information. When encountering a questionable post on social media, the easiest action is to simply ignore it. By not clicking and not re-posting, every reader can play a part in reducing the viral spread of false theories.

Another option is to have a conversation with the person who posted the false theory. Friends and family members can talk to each other about how important it is to fact-check information and to avoid spreading unfounded theories. However, it is important to stay respectful and kind at all times. If a family member or friend finds it frustrating to talk with the conspiracy theorist, and if there is no real harm in it, the best solution is often to just ignore it. (Of course, you should always talk to a trusted adult before posting on social media. Furthermore, you should not engage in online conversations with someone you don't know.)

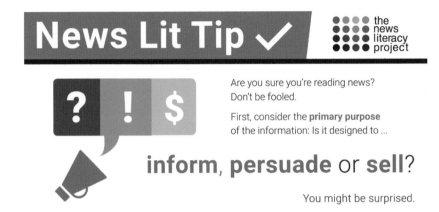

News Lit Tip ✓

the news literacy project

Are you sure you're reading news? Don't be fooled.

First, consider the **primary purpose** of the information: Is it designed to ...

inform, persuade or sell?

You might be surprised.

The News Literacy Project teaches how to think about the credibility of news and other articles.

Sometimes a bit of your own research can turn up accurate information that you can then share with the conspiracy theorist, but there is no guarantee that the person will feel comfortable hearing it. Since people who feel like they don't have power are more likely to believe in superstitions and conspiracy theories, a rational approach may not be effective. Sometimes being a good listener and making someone feel important and empowered will reduce their conspiracy-related inclinations more than arguing with them.

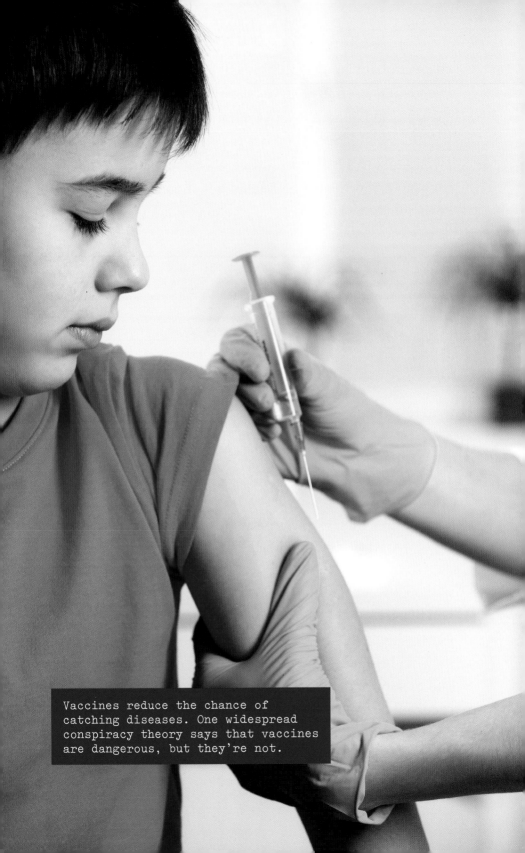

Vaccines reduce the chance of catching diseases. One widespread conspiracy theory says that vaccines are dangerous, but they're not.

Putting Your Skills into Action

n general, there are some traits that help readers to trust information from certain sources. For instance, a trustworthy news source will explain where it got its information. It will publish corrections if mistakes were made or publish an update when needed. It will also use a tone of respect, and not write in an insulting or shocking way. Let's look at some examples.

Using CARS to Fact-Check

Librarians, teachers, and other information experts have made some guidelines to help students and others know if a source of information can be trusted. You can remember these guidelines by the acronym "CARS." C stands for credibility, A stands for accuracy, R stands for reasonableness, and S stands for sources.

C Is for Credibility

The first question to ask yourself is, who do you trust to tell you reliable information? Parents are often good people to ask, but as students grow older, they might have questions their parents cannot answer.

For example, if you want to know what is best for your health, a doctor or health care provider is usually a good source. Your local health department is also a good place to find accurate information about your health. If you want to know if vaccines are safe, it is wise to ask someone who studies this as part of his or her job. A good doctor will be able to tell you about the real risks of any medical treatment.

If you want to check for online sources of information, try to find articles or web pages from well-established places such as a well-known research hospital or university. Most adults have heard of Harvard Medical School or the Mayo Clinic. Be skeptical of websites that sell products like vitamins. Their main goal might be to make money instead of to share the truth.

The United States and Canada both provide a lot of good quality medical information on government websites. You can recognize a United States government website because the web address or URL ends with ".gov." Canadian government web sources are found at http://www.canada.ca. For example, health information from the Canadian government can be found at https://www.canada.ca/en/health-canada.

Make sure your information comes from trustworthy organizations. The Mayo Clinic is a trusted source of health information.

A respected US government website about health is http://www.medlineplus.gov. This site is run by the US National Library of Medicine. Many doctors and scientists check the information to make sure it is the very best available to the American public. If you have a medical question, you can type some keywords into the search bar and find good quality information about the topic. Try typing in the words "vaccine autism," and see what you find. You will find links to hundreds of articles about this topic. The links go to respected websites like the Mayo Clinic and organizations that work on children's health. The linked organizations have all studied this topic carefully to find the best answers. If you aren't sure about one source, you can read more than one and compare them to each other.

A Is for Accuracy

One question to ask when it comes to science and medicine is: How old is this information? New research is being done every day, so it is important to check that the information you are using is the most recent or current. If you are reading an article from several years ago, it is a good idea to check to see if the information has been updated within the past two or three years. When it comes to science and medicine, information can become out of date quickly.

On the other hand, historical information remains true, so older sources may be just as valid as newer ones, depending on your topic. Articles about literature, philosophy, and art can stand the test of time.

A second question to ask is whether this source gets updated or fact-checked regularly. Good quality news sources will correct their mistakes and let readers know.

R Is for Reasonableness

Does the story sound reasonable? Can a reader detect any bias, or taking one side over the other? If the source is an organization with a specific goal or purpose, it might publish only material that supports its goal.

Is it fair? Does the website or news source seem to be trying to persuade the reader to take a certain view, or does it allow the reader to decide for herself or himself how to interpret the facts? If an article sounds unbelievable, check it against other sources.

S Is for Sources

Finally, ask yourself if the article or website you are looking at shows its work. A good article will include references, notes, or a bibliography. This shows that the author is not inventing the information. A website will often include hyperlinks. You can click on the links to find more information about the topic. If the links go to disreputable websites or online stores, you should not trust the article.

Thinking Through Vaccinations and Autism

The theory that vaccinations cause autism is very common and has real-world consequences for public health. The theory was started in 1998 by one man, Dr. Andrew Wakefield. Dr. Wakefield published a single study suggesting there was a connection between vaccines and autism. For the next ten years, many researchers tested this claim. In all, they studied more than twenty-five million children in dozens of studies and found no connection. It turns out that doctor Wakefield's study had tested only twelve children and did not use the best-proven research methods.

Even though Wakefield's theory has been tested carefully by scientists and proved false, many parents still fear giving their children vaccines. Even President Trump has mentioned this conspiracy as if it were true. As a result, children's health is put at risk. In 2012, almost fifty thousand cases of whooping cough (also called pertussis) appeared in the United States. Whooping cough lasts about ten weeks and

In 1998, a doctor named Andrew Wakefield spread a false story that vaccines cause autism in children.

JACOB ABRAMS, CONSPIRACY THEORIES, AND THE FIRST AMENDMENT

In the early 1900s, a man named Jacob Abrams believed that the United States government had conspired with capitalists to play a role in the Russian Revolution. Abrams was an anarchist, or a person who does not believe in government.

Long before the internet existed, Abrams wished to share his theory with others. He found a small printing press and published leaflets, or small pamphlets, about his conspiracy theory. He and his friends climbed to the third floor of a Manhattan building and dropped the leaflets down on the people below. Unfortunately for Abrams and his colleagues, they were charged with inciting resistance to the war effort and sentenced to prison. The Supreme Court ruled against them in 1919 in the case of *Abrams v. United States*. They were charged under the Espionage Act of 1917. Although the court ruled against Abrams and the others, Justice Oliver Wendell Holmes disagreed with the decision. He and Justice Brandeis stated that these defendants were not a risk. Holmes and Brandeis believed they should have been protected under the First Amendment, which guarantees the freedom of speech. Freedom of speech is one reason that conspiracy theories flourish. However, protecting the First Amendment is critical to democracy in the United States. This is why media literacy skills will never go out of style.

The Centers for Disease Control is where the best doctors, researchers, and experts work together to try to limit the spread of disease to the public.

can be life-threatening in babies. According to the CDC, several recent outbreaks of measles in recent years have also spread among unvaccinated communities.

The autism theory was first proposed decades ago. It came about because many children were diagnosed with autism at about eighteen months of age. This was also the age at which children were likely to have received vaccinations. Sometimes when two different things happen at the same time, it is because one thing causes the other. But more often, the two events have no link. At times, both of the events could be caused by a third factor that has not even been considered. This is called a correlation, which means two events seem to be related, but the nature of the relationship is not known.

Scientists use careful methods to try to test whether there is a cause-and-effect relationship between two correlated events. When doctors, scientists, and researchers first learned of Wakefield's concern, they immediately set to work to test what kind of relationship there might be between vaccines and autism. After many years of experiments, reputable scientists have determined that vaccines do not cause autism. The real cause of autism is still not known for sure, so scientists are hard at work conducting new research about autism.

Still, some groups continue to claim that vaccines cause autism in children. These people might not be aware of the research studies that have proven that theory to be false. Instead, they base their ideas on old or false information. Some of these people know a little bit about science but do not understand the newest information.

There is a lot at stake if many people believe this conspiracy theory and choose not to vaccinate children. When vaccination rates go down, more people can get sick from preventable diseases. Sadly, the people most likely to get sick are young children, the elderly, and people with weak immune systems. A few people have special conditions that make vaccines risky for them, so they are not able to receive the shots. If most other people around them are vaccinated, these people will be safe due to what is known as herd immunity. However, if many others don't receive vaccines, then the chance of at-risk populations getting sick goes up.

Many news and government sources have reported on the rise of illnesses such as measles, mumps, and whooping cough since the early 2000s. They also have reported on the safety of vaccines. An article published in *Medical Daily* in 2014 summarizes the research that has been done on this. The Centers for Disease Control provides information about vaccines, outbreaks, and symptoms of these and other diseases.

A Closer Look at the "Faked" Moon Landing

Historians tell us that in 1969, Neil Armstrong was the first human being to walk on the moon. Many people of older generations, such as grandparents and great-grandparents, remember watching the film footage on television. Between 1969 and 1972, twelve people walked on the moon.

A popular conspiracy theory found on the internet states that the first moon landing was faked. According to this theory, the film footage was made not on the moon but in a Hollywood studio. One YouTube video shows the film footage itself and says that the shadows and waving flag are not realistic.

How should a skeptical thinker go about evaluating this conspiracy theory about the moon landing?

Credibility

First, a reader might think about the kind of sources that promote this conspiracy theory. There are many websites that have articles related

Twelve astronauts have set foot on the moon. One conspiracy theory says that all moon landings were faked. However, there is a huge amount of evidence that proves the moon landings took place.

to this conspiracy. One of the most famous people who question the moon landing is Marcus Allen. Allen is a British man who publishes an "alternative news" magazine called Nexus. He has spoken about how he believes NASA is lying. Recently, he talked at a conference about the paranormal, conspiracy theories, alternative thought, and new age philosophy.

Another person who thinks the moon landing was faked is an American named Bart Sibrel. Sibrel believes the CIA organized the hoax in order to distract Americans from the Vietnam War. Sibrel is not a scientist. He is a photographer and videographer on a mission to disprove the moon landing. The opening of his film called *A Funny Thing Happened on the Way to the Moon* mixes together science, religion, and mythology.

Accuracy

Marcus Allen, Bart Sibrel, and other conspiracy theorists who write about the moon landing topic are not scientists. Allen and Sibrel both mention a real problem of space travel called the Van Allen belts. These two belts of radiation were discovered in 1958 and created a real challenge for astronauts heading toward the moon. The belts were named after James Van Allen, the scientist who studied the radiation data. Allen, Sibrel and others claim that the belts are impossible to pass through. But many scientists who study them—including Van Allen—say the problem is not passing through but avoiding too much radiation. According to scientists with NASA and professors of physics and astronomy, the problem of the

Van Allen belts was solved. Astronauts had to navigate through the least dangerous path of the belts and also passed through quickly in order to avoid too much radiation exposure.

Apart from the Van Allen belts, Sibrel and others mostly rely on images to support their theories. They have shown unverified images and film footage to raise doubts about the moon landing.

Reasonableness and Logical Thinking

If one looks at the big picture, beyond the film footage and individual facts, the "faked moon landing" conspiracy theory breaks down. For example, thousands of people were involved in the Apollo project, and they all have memories and records of the great work they did in order to first send a man to the moon. Reams of evidence related to the space launch still exist. The many mathematicians who calculated the complex formulas, engineers who built the necessary equipment, and even janitorial and other support staff all witnessed the long project from beginning to end. Private contractors had to build the equipment. Their stories are numerous. It is very unlikely that thousands of people would be willing to keep the hoax a secret for all these decades.

According to an article in the March 2018 *National Geographic*, twelve people have walked on the moon so far. These people are from several different countries and have gone there at different times. In addition, more than four hundred astronauts have spent time in space, including in orbit, traveling to the moon, and living on the

International Space Station. Thousands of people from all around the world worked together to make the space missions succeed. The more we look at the bigger picture, the less credibility the conspiracy theory has.

Sources

A quick Google search with the keywords "moon landing was faked" shows many familiar sources that debunk this theory rather than support it. Familiar and respected sources like *National Geographic*, *Time Magazine*, *Snopes*, *Newsweek*, and *Popular Mechanics* have checked out this theory and debunked it already.

What's at Stake?

At first glance, perhaps it would seem that the "faked moon landing" is a harmless belief. It doesn't have the same consequences as if people were to stop getting vaccinations and cause epidemics of disease. On the other hand, people who think that the space program is a lie will not want to use tax dollars to fund research in the future. Research in the space program has led to many benefits for ordinary people like GPS devices, which help us to navigate. It is also connected to the creation of many products and medical devices that improve quality of life.

Choose Your Own Conspiracy Theory

Think of a conspiracy theory that you have heard of through a friend, family member, or the media. Use the following steps to think through or write about how you might debunk it.

According to the United Nations Office for Outer Space Affairs, more than 4,800 satellites were orbiting Earth in early 2018. Satellites give us important scientific evidence about space.

1. Who told you about this theory? What evidence did they provide? Why might they believe it?

2. What do other sources that you trust say about this theory? (Find at least three different sources that come from trained experts.)

3. What would happen if many people believed in this theory instead of trusting in the commonly accepted view?

4. Complete an internet search to find at least three articles about this topic. Check each article to see how credible it is. (Do they use names and studies to support their claims? Do they fact-check their information? Do they publish corrections? Is anyone watching over this organization to make sure they are using best practices in journalism?)

5. What products are being advertised on these websites? What other articles are published on the site? Does it make sense? Do they use extreme or shocking language in their headlines?

It's OK to Be a Skeptic

Nicolas Fillion is a philosophy professor at Simon Fraser University in British Columbia, Canada. He teaches a course on conspiracy theories. As part of his research, he studies conspiracy websites. He is a conspiracy theory theorist—someone who works on theories about conspiracy theories! He emphasizes that the difference between science and pseudoscience is "falsifiability." This means that a theory has to be testable. If the theory cannot be tested, it cannot be proven. He says that conspiracy theories are not crazy. Fillion told reporter Yan Barcelo, "I think that it's part of a sane attitude to entertain the possibility of conspiracies. In these times of potential control and surveillance, a certain level of alertness and suspicion is indicated."

Therefore, all readers are wise to be alert and skeptical about the sources they read. Critical thinking and evaluation are important skills to develop. Everything should be examined with a cautious eye—including conspiracy theories themselves.

CONSPIRACY THEORIES ABOUT SCHOOL SHOOTINGS

On Valentine's Day in 2018, a young man attacked a Parkland, Florida, high school. He shot and killed seventeen students and teachers. Many others were injured. Right away, students at the school who survived the shooting began to speak out about the need for better laws about guns. They posted videos on social media, conducted peaceful protests, and met with lawmakers to ask for safer laws.

The following week, some people began to claim that the students in the videos were not real students but actors who were paid to pretend to be students. These people called the students "crisis actors." In reality, crisis actors are people who pretend to be victims during training exercises for the police and military. The term was misapplied to these high schoolers. Conspiracy theorists said the students were actors who were paid to pretend to have been at the event. These claims were easily debunked by the students' teachers, family, friends, and reporters. Still, the fake story kept spreading on YouTube.

The *Los Angeles Times*, BBC, and other news sources reported on this and other conspiracy theories that cropped up during the week following the school shooting. According to that reporting, one reason the "crisis actor" conspiracy theory spread so quickly was because of Facebook and YouTube, which use nonhuman algorithms to promote some stories over others. A flaw in the algorithm made conspiracy videos go viral.

GLOSSARY

algorithm A set of instructions or rules used by computers.

bias An unfair slant toward one view or group at the expense of the other side.

code of ethics A set of rules created to help guide an organization to make good, responsible choices.

conspiracy theory An unproven belief that two or more people are working together to fool others, often in a complex way.

contradict To show that the opposite is true.

correlation A relationship that exists between two different things, but whether it is a direct cause-and-effect relationship is unclear.

credibility The degree to which something or someone can be believed.

crisis actor Someone hired to play the role of a victim in training exercises for police or military. Some conspiracy theorists have misapplied this term to real victims and survivors of shootings.

evaluate To determine the significance or value of something.

First Amendment An addition to the United States Constitution that guarantees freedom of speech, which means that people can speak their opinions and views without punishment.

logical fallacy A fault or flaw in an otherwise reasonable explanation.

paratext Material found around or near a text, whether online or in print.

rationale A part of an argument that explains the connection between the facts and the claim.

reliability A term for how consistently the same results can be achieved from the same test or experiment.

skeptical A description of someone who asks what is true rather than blindly accepting what they see or read.

FURTHER INFORMATION

Books

Cunningham, Darryl. *How to Fake a Moon Landing: Exposing the Myths of Science Denial.* New York: Abrams ComicArts, 2013.

Palser, Barb. *Choosing News: What Gets Reported and Why.* Mankato, NY: Compass Point Books, 2012.

Websites

Checkology Digital Classroom
http://www.thenewsliteracyproject.org/services/checkology

Use this comprehensive resource from the News Literacy Project to help evaluate the quality of news and other media sources.

Digital Resource Center: Center for News Literacy
http://drc.centerfornewsliteracy.org

This website is hosted by the Stony Brook University School of Journalism and provides tools and resources to help students and teachers learn about news literacy. It includes a short online course that covers the basics of news literacy for students.

Factitious

http://factitious.augamestudio.com

Factitious is a free interactive online game that provides short articles and asks readers to guess whether they are real news or fake news.

NewseumED

https://newseumed.org/stack/media-literacy-resources

This site provides activities and tools for teachers and students to help build news literacy skills.

Videos

Bill Nye on Conspiracy Theorists: NASA's Moon Landing, Vaccines, Astrology, and Tarot Cards

https://www.youtube.com/watch?v=MFLtTK13G2w

Scientist Bill Nye explains one approach to take when discussing divisive topics with a conspiracy theorists.

How to Choose Your News

https://ed.ted.com/lessons/how-to-choose-your-news-damon-brown

In this short video, educator Damon Brown explains the many sources of news and information available today and offers suggestions for managing and evaluating those sources.

BIBLIOGRAPHY

Barcelo, Yan. "The Truth You Don't Know." *CPA Magazine*, September 1, 2017. https://www.cpacanada.ca/en/connecting-and-news/cpa-magazine/articles/2017/september/the-truth-you-dont-know.

Center for News Literacy: Stony Brook University School of Journalism. "Getting Started." Retrieved March 1, 2018. http://www.centerfornewsliteracy.org/getting-started.

Filucci, Sierra. "How to Spot Fake News (and Teach Kids to be Media Savvy)." Common Sense Media, March 20, 2017. https://www.commonsensemedia.org/blog/how-to-spot-fake-news-and-teach-kids-to-be-media-savvy?utm_source=twitter&utm_medium=social.

Hogenboom, Melissa. "The Enduring Appeal of Conspiracy Theories." BBC, January 24, 2018. http://www.bbc.com/future/story/20180124-the-enduring-appeal-of-conspiracy-theories.

James Madison University Libraries. "Media & News Literacy: News Literacy." Updated December 18, 2017. http://guides.lib.jmu.edu/medialiteracy/news.

Meyer, David. "YouTube Enlists Wikipedia in its Conspiracy Theory Crackdown. But That Might Not

Be Enough." *Fortune*, March 14, 2018. http://fortune.com/2018/03/14/youtube-conspiracy-theory-wikipedia.

News Literacy Project (NLP). "Program." Retrieved March 1, 2018. http://www.thenewsliteracyproject.org/about/program.

Olmsted, Kathryn S. *Real Enemies: Conspiracy Theories and American Democracy, World War I to 9/11*. London, UK: Oxford University Press, 2009.

Poynter Institute. "International Fact-Checking Network Fact-Checkers' Code of Principles." Retrieved March 1, 2018. https://www.poynter.org/international-fact-checking-network-fact-checkers-code-principles.

Shermer, Michael, and Pat Linse. "Conspiracy Theories: Who Believes Them and Why, and How to Determine if a Conspiracy Theory is True or False." Skeptics Society. Retrieved March 1, 2018. https://www.skeptic.com/downloads/conspiracy-theories-who-why-and-how.pdf.

Solon, Olivia. "YouTube Will Use Wikipedia to Help Solve its Conspiracy Theory Problem." *Guardian*, March 13, 2018. https://www.theguardian.com/technology/2018/mar/13/youtube-wikipedia-flag-conspiracy-theory-videos.

Spinner, Jackie. "Study: Educating News Consumers About the Media Can Curb Conspiracy Theory Appeal." *Columbia Journalism Review*, December 20, 2017. https://www.cjr.org/united_states_project/news-media-literacy-conspiracy-theory.php.

INDEX

ABOUT THE AUTHOR

Anna Maria Johnson teaches courses in writing, research, and the humanities at James Madison University. She also writes and edits books and essays for a variety of audiences, ranging from elementary school to the graduate school level. Johnson lives near Harrisonburg, Virginia, with her husband and their two teenage daughters. Her favorite hobbies include reading, listening to people's stories, and thinking about different points of view.